Pebble Plus

SEA LIFE

REGAL TANGS

by **Mari Schuh**

Consulting Editor:
Gail Saunders-Smith, PhD

Consultant:
Jody Rake, Member,
Southwest Marine Educators Association

CAPSTONE PRESS
a capstone imprint

Pebble Plus is published by Capstone Press,
1710 Roe Crest Drive, North Mankato, Minnesota 56003
www.capstonepub.com

Library of Congress Cataloging-in-Publication Data
Cataloging-in-publication information is on file with the Library of Congress.
ISBN 978-1-4914-6041-2 (library binding)
ISBN 978-1-4914-6061-0 (eBook PDF)

Editorial Credits
Elizabeth R. Johnson, editor; Aruna Rangarajan, designer;
Kelly Garvin, media researcher; Tori Abraham, production specialist

Photo Credits
Regal Tangs photo credits
Alamy/Roberto Nistri, 21; Dreamstime/Lukas Blazek, 5, Glow Images/ImageBROKER, 17; iStockphoto/mirecca, 15; Shutterstock: artefacti, 8, bluehand, cover, Brad Barkel, 9, Dobermaraner, 13, Godruma, cover (background), Johanna Goodyear, 11, Peter Leahy, 19; Superstock/imageBROKER, 7

Design Elements: Shutterstock: SusIO, Vectomart

Note to Parents and Teachers

The Sea Life set supports national science standards related to life science. This book describes and illustrates regal tangs. The images support early readers in understanding the text. The repetition of words and phrases helps early readers learn new words. This book also introduces early readers to subject-specific vocabulary words, which are defined in the Glossary section. Early readers may need assistance to read some words and to use the Table of Contents, Glossary, Read More, Internet Sites, and Index sections of the book.

Printed in China by Nordica
0415/CA21500542
032015   008837NORDF15

Table of Contents

What's a Regal Tang?

Regal tangs have a secret. Sharp spines pop out from their tails when they're attacked. These fish are called surgeonfish because they can cut like a surgeon!

spine

Regal tangs have many names.
They are called palette surgeonfish,
Pacific blue tangs, and hippo tangs.

Regal tangs live in the Indian
and Pacific oceans.
They swim in warm water
near coral reefs.

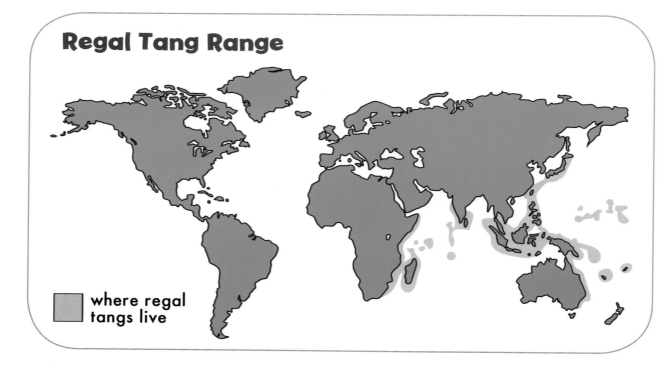

Regal Tang Range

where regal
tangs live

Up Close

Regal tangs are oval-shaped.
They have flat bodies.
They can grow to 12 inches
(30 centimeters) long.

Regal tangs are bright blue
with black markings.
Small scales cover their bodies.
Their tails are yellow.

Finding Food

Regal tangs often eat
in small groups.
They use their sharp teeth to
pick algae off rocks and coral.

Growing Up

Regal tangs hatch from their
eggs after about one day.
The larvae grow quickly.
After one week, scales form
on their bodies.

Young regal tangs are yellow.
They turn blue as they get older.
Regal tangs live up to 30 years
in the wild.

Staying Safe

Regal tangs try to hide to stay safe. They use their spines if they are attacked. These beautiful fish can defend themselves.

Glossary

algae—small plants without roots or stems that grow in water

coral reef—a type of land close to the surface of the ocean made up of the hardened bodies of corals; corals are small, colorful sea creatures

defend—to protect something or someone from harm

hatch—to break out of an egg

larva—an animal at the stage of development between an egg and an adult; more than one larva are larvae

scale—one of the small, thin plates that cover the bodies of fish

spine—a hard, sharp, pointed growth on an animal's body

Read More

Hansen, Grace. *Tropical Fish.* Ocean Life. Minneapolis: Abdo Kids, 2015.

Hughes, Catherine D. *First Big Book of the Ocean.* National Geographic Little Kids. Washington, D.C.: National Geographic Kids, 2013.

Martin, Isabel. *Fish: A Question and Answer Book.* Animal Kingdom Questions and Answers. North Mankato, Minn.: Capstone Press, 2015.

Internet Sites

FactHound offers a safe, fun way to find Internet sites related to this book. All of the sites on FactHound have been researched by our staff.

Here's all you do:

Visit www.facthound.com

Type in this code: 9781491460412

Super-cool stuff!

Check out projects, games and lots more at
www.capstonekids.com

Index

Word Count: 180

Grade: 1

Early-Intervention Level: 14